spot

BACKYARD ANIMALS

BATS

by Wendy Strobel Dieker

AMICUS | AMICUS INK

wings

teeth

Look for these words and pictures as you read.

ears

feet

The sun is setting.
Bats fly out of their home.

Do you see its wings?
A bat is a flying mammal.

wings

Do you see its eyes?
Bats do not see well.
How does a bat find food?

ears

Do you see its big ears?
The bat hears where bugs are.

teeth

Do you see its teeth?
Chomp! Bats eat the bugs.

feet

Do you see its feet?
Bats hang upside down.

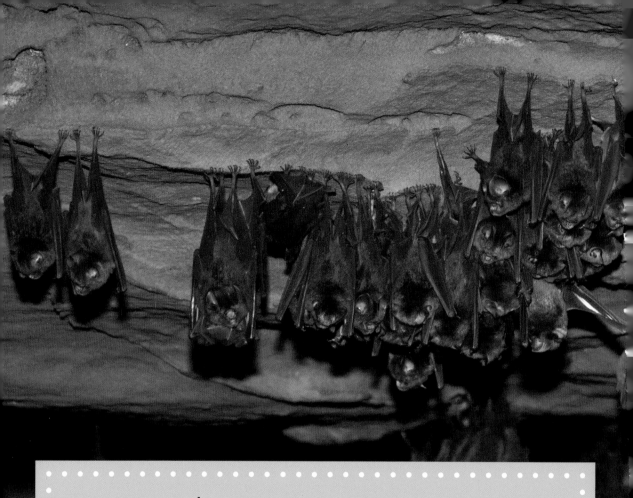

The sun comes up.
The bats gather in a dark place.
Sleep tight, bats.

Do you see its wings?
A bat is a flying mammal.

wings

teeth

Do you see its teeth?
Chomp! Bats eat the bugs.

wings

teeth

Did you find?

ears

feet

ears

Do you see its big ears?
The bat hears where bugs are.

feet

Do you see its feet?
Bats hang upside down.

Spot is published by Amicus and Amicus Ink
P.O. Box 1329, Mankato, MN 56002
www.amicuspublishing.us

Library of Congress Cataloging-in-Publication Data
Names: Dieker, Wendy Strobel.
Title: Bats / by Wendy Strobel Dieker.
Description: Mankato, Minnesota : Amicus, 2018. | Series:
  Spot. Backyard animals | Audience: Grades K to 3.
Identifiers: LCCN 2016044419 (print) | LCCN 2017000726
  (ebook) | ISBN 9781681510903 (library binding) | ISBN
  9781681511801 (e-book) | ISBN 9781681522159 (pbk.)
Subjects: LCSH: Bats--Juvenile literature.
Classification: LCC QL737.C5 D54 2018 (print) | LCC
  QL737.C5 (ebook) | DDC 599.4--dc23
LC record available at https://lccn.loc.gov/2016044419

Printed in the United States of America

HC 10 9 8 7 6 5 4 3 2 1
PB 10 9 8 7 6 5 4 3 2 1

Rebecca Glaser, editor
Deb Miner, series designer
Ciara Beitlich, book designer
Holly Young, photo researcher

Photos by AgeFotoStock 1; Alamy
Stock Photo 4–5, 6–7, 12–13, 14–15;
Getty Images 3; Shutterstock cover,
8–9, 10–11

BATS